Cornwall Beach and Cove Guide
North Coast

Robert Hesketh

Bossiney Books • Exeter

First published 2021 by
Bossiney Books Ltd, 68 Thorndale Courts, Whitycombe Way,
Exeter, EX4 2NY
www.bossineybooks.com
© 2021 Robert Hesketh All rights reserved
ISBN 978-1-906474-89-8

Acknowledgements
The maps are by Graham Hallowell
All photographs are by the author, www.roberthesketh.co.uk
or from the publisher's own collection

Printed in Great Britain by Booths Print, Penryn, Cornwall

Introduction

Cornwall's north coast offers 236 km (147 miles) of remarkably varied natural beauty. From miles of golden sand washed by surf-capped Atlantic waves to charming harbours and secluded rocky coves, Cornwall is endlessly enjoyable. Whether you're looking for swimming, surfing, scenery, water sports, amusing the children, walking the dog, or just lazing in the sun, this guide is designed to help you find what you want. Practical information, including parking, access and lifeguard cover, as well as facilities such as beach cafés, shops and toilets are given to help you choose from 75 beaches and coves.

Beach safety

Cornwall's beaches are delightful and safe places – provided beach users take responsibility for their safety and a few simple common sense precautions are followed, especially with children. Tides and currents affect all beaches, but some much more than others. Please check tide times, heed warning notices and advice from lifeguards and keep well within the limits of your strength and skill.

Avoid swimming, surfing or boating alone or in rough seas. Observe posted warnings of dangerous currents. Do not swim if the red flag is flying or in zones covered by the black and white flag (watercraft only). On lifeguarded beaches, swim between the red/yellow flags. Some beaches have seasonal lifeguard cover as shown in this book. In emergency, call the Coastguard on 999.

Other potential hazards that can be readily avoided include being cut off on isolated beaches by the tide; drifting out to sea on inflatable boats (never use them if the orange windsock is flying, it indicates offshore winds); slipping on wet rocks and steep paths (wear shoes); and tunnelling deeply into soft sand, which can collapse. On certain beaches, rock falls are a potential hazard, but only directly under unstable cliffs. Please heed warning notices. Equally, keep away from cliff edges if exploring the Coast Path.

Seashore code

Please do your bit towards protecting Cornwall's wonderful coasts.
Take litter home.
Return all live specimens – crabs, prawns etc – to the water.
Replace seaweeds and rocks where you find them.
Report anything unusual.

Tides

North Cornwall's beaches have a huge tidal difference, so it's wise to check tide times (available online) before planning your trip. Whilst Cornish beaches may be huge at low tide, high tide shrinks them to a fraction of their full size. Some even become completely submerged.

Access

Ease of access to Cornish beaches varies considerably. Generally, the more accessible beaches have better facilities and are much busier than beaches that are harder to reach: but these secluded places have a charm of their own. We have indicated where care, time, effort and agility are needed to access a beach.

Key to symbols used

P	Parking
P	Free parking (at the time of writing)
WC	Toilets
△	Sandy beach
⚐	Surfing popular – but not necessarily safe!
✸	Lifeguards (seasonal only)
🐕	Dogs banned (sometimes summer only)
🐕	Dogs permitted all year (at the time of writing)
🐕	Dogs permitted with restrictions
✕	Café
⚲	Pub or bar fairly near
⬛	Shop(s)
⚘	Wildlife
⌒	Fishing
♿	Disabled access

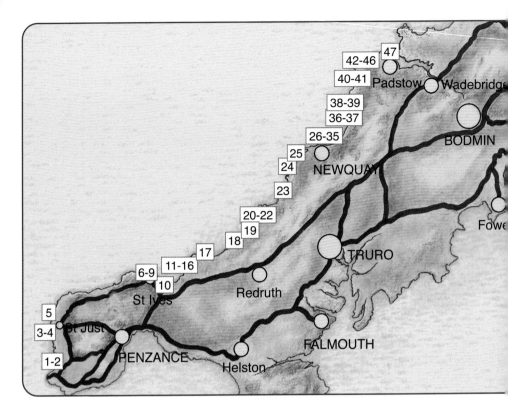

Land's End to Padstow

Cornwall's north coast is well known for water sports, especially surfing. Many of its famous surfing beaches, including Cornwall's surfing capital, Newquay, as well as Sennen, Perran Sands, Mawgan Porth, Constantine and Harlyn Bays, are also great family beaches with good swimming and fine sand to delight children. Most are lifeguarded with excellent facilities. With so much to offer they naturally attract many people, but as the tide draws back, revealing rock pools and sea caves, they grow exponentially and have room for everyone.

In sharp contrast to these beaches exposed to the force of the restless ocean, St Ives' sheltered harbour and Porthminster beaches get the full benefit of Cornwall's mild climate. Several coves tucked in among cliffs, such as Fishing Cove and Porth Ledden, are similarly sheltered. These are places for peace and contemplation and are well worth the walk to reach them.

1 Sennen Cove

Nets, lines and crab pots are stacked by Sennen's small harbour car park. Fishing boats were formerly hauled up the slipway by the capstan housed in the Roundhouse and Capstan Gallery, home to art in various media.

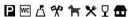

2 Whitesand Bay

The Bay's 2 km (1¼ miles) of golden sands are ideal for families. It is also famous for surfing. There is a good choice of refreshments along Sennen's smart sea front as well as a beach bar. During the season, dogs are only permitted at the north end of the beach.

3 Porth Nanven a.k.a. Cot Beach

The 'Dinosaur Egg Beach' has large rounded boulders which were shaped by the sea 120,000 years ago. It is relatively quiet and secluded, but exploring it calls for some agility. There is sand at low tide, but beware metal sherds if paddling. Use the small car park 2 km (1½ miles) west of St Just at the end of the Cot Valley (SW357309).

4 Priest's Cove

This small, rocky cove below Cape Cornwall offers a little sand at low tide and a tidal pool, perfect for learning to swim. Dolphins, seals and basking sharks are often seen from here and neighbouring coves. Access is a fairly steep five minute walk from the car park (facilities).

5 Porth Ledden

Tucked under the cliffs on the north side of Cape Cornwall, Porth Ledden is a lovely rocky cove. Not well known, it's good for solitude, walking the dog and rockpooling, but only accessible at low tide and after a ten minute walk from the car park. Some agility is needed on the damaged slipway and wet rocks.

🅿 🆆 🐕 ✖ 🐓

6 Porthmeor Beach, St Ives

A large, beautiful sandy beach, Porthmeor has excellent facilities, combined with easy access from two car parks (ramp at the western end, steps at the eastern end). Lifeguarded and family friendly, it has a surf school and shop. With so much to offer, Porthmeor and neighbouring beaches are always popular.

🅿 🆆 ⛺ 🏄 🎣 🐕 ✖ 🍺 🏠 ♿

7 Porthgwidden Beach, St Ives

Porthgwidden is a popular family beach. Similar to, but smaller, more sheltered and with gentler waves than neighbouring Porthmeor beach, it too has golden sand and excellent facilities, but no lifeguard. The car park is right by. Approach down steps or a steep ramp.

🅿 🆆 ⛺ 🐕 ✖ 🍺 🏠

8 Harbour Beach, St Ives

St Ives's harbour beach is a sheltered suntrap, ideal for a stroll along Smeaton's Pier. Stop by a café, pub, gallery or shop. Watch fishermen land their catch, laze on a deckchair, paddle in the shallow water, build a sandcastle with the children, take a boat or fishing trip. At low tide, it forms one vast stretch of sand with Porthminster beach. There's a seasonal dog ban, except for the sandy extension north of the pier (Bamaluz Beach, covered at high tide).

9 Porthminster Beach, St Ives

Porthminster is a Blue Flag beach of golden sand in an azure sea with wonderful views of St Ives harbour and across St Ives Bay to Godrevy lighthouse. Ideal for families, it is lifeguarded with safe swimming and a nearby mini golf course. St Ives has many facilities. Access is down steps from the railway station car park. Parking in St Ives is expensive and can be difficult. The railway park-and-ride from St Erth is a popular alternative.

10 Carbis Bay

This beautiful Blue Flag beach is great for families and for swimming, kayaking and canoeing, but not for surfing. Beware currents near Carrick Gladden (Hawk's Point) at the east end of the beach. Lifeguarded, it has a convenient rail station (park and ride at St Erth), beach hut hire, car park, toilets and café.

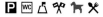

11 Porth Kidney Sands

At low tide, this is a vast area of sands, ideal for dogs. Access is via the Coast Path from Lelant church (limited free roadside parking) or Carbis Bay car park (toilets and a café). Surfing is popular, but somewhat tricky. Beware strong currents around the Hayle estuary.

🅿 🅿 ᵂᶜ ⛺ 🏄 🐕 ✕ 🐦

12 Hayle Towans and Mexico Towans Beaches

As the tide drops, Hayle Towans (from *tewynn*, Cornish for dunes) forms three miles of golden sand and dunes, continuous with Gwithian and Godrevy beaches. This gives ample space for surfers and families, with rock pools and sand pools. Conditions are ideal for sand yachts and kite buggies. Swimming is good, but beware dangerous currents in the Hayle estuary. There is a seasonal dog ban, but dogs are allowed further east along the beach at Mexico Towans.

🅿 ᵂᶜ ⛺ 🧍 🏄 🐕 ✕ ♿

13 Gwithian Towans

A huge sand and surf beach with good facilities, Gwithian Towans is lifeguarded and popular with surfers and kitesurfers, whilst families enjoy the rockpools and the firm sand (great for sandcastles). The beach is zoned for swimming, surfing and dogs. Please follow the signs and warnings at the beach entrance, a short walk from the car park and down steps. The 400 ha (960 acres) of dunes behind the Hayle and Gwithian beaches are very rich in wildlife (see plaque in car park).

🅿 ᵂᶜ ⛺ 🧍 🏄 🐕 🐕 ✕ ♿ 🐦

14 Godrevy Towans

A short, level walk through the dunes from either the café car park or the small free parking area by the chimney leads to Godrevy's vast sandy beach, also accessible from the lower National Trust car park. Great for a family day out, it's lifeguarded and zoned for swimming and surfing. The surf school by the café offers equipment hire and lessons.

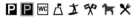

15 Godrevy Cove

A beach of sand and rocks, with good rockpools, Godrevy Cove is accessible from the further National Trust car park. It forms one huge beach with Godrevy Towans and Gwithian Towans at low tide – be careful not to be caught when it rises! Access is via steps. At the north end is Godrevy lighthouse.

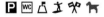

16 Mutton Cove

A short, well-surfaced walk from Godrevy car park, Mutton Cove is the most likely place to see seals in Cornwall; they sometimes gather in numbers on the beach. The beach itself is inaccessible (to humans), but it's also a great place to watch seabirds and dolphins. The Coast Path and neighbouring coastal heath and grass are a rich bird habitat, not least for larks. Please keep behind the rails, avoid unnecessary noise, and keep dogs on leads.

9

17 Fishing Cove

A lovely secluded, sheltered sandy beach, Fishing Cove (a naturist beach) is not widely known. It's unsigned and access calls for some effort and agility on a steep descent, aided by steps and rope guides. Use the most westerly North Cliff car park between Gwithian and Hell's Mouth (SW 599427). Follow the path west for 100m. Continue for 150m on the Coastpath. Turn right onto a narrow path through scrub to the beach path.

P 🛁 🐕

18 Portreath

Portreath's mostly sandy beach benefits from a convenient car park, disabled access and good facilities, including cafés, shops, pubs and an amusement arcade. It is lifeguarded and good for families and surfers alike. Formerly a busy port exporting local ores to South Wales for smelting, Portreath retains its small harbour behind the beach.

P WC 🛁 🧗 🏄 🐕 ✕ 🍺 🚌 ♿

19 Porthtowan

A beach of golden sand backed by dunes, Porthtowan is popular with both surfers and families. It is lifeguarded and zoned with easy access and good facilities, including a surf shop and paddle board hire, plus a children's play area. Low tide gives access to Chapel Porth beach.

P WC 🛁 🧗 🏄 🐕 ✕ 🍺 🚌 ♿

20 Chapel Porth

A rock and shingle cove which becomes a large beach of golden sand with rock pools and caves to explore as the tide drops. Lifeguarded, it is appreciated by families and surfers alike. There is convenient beach parking, café and toilets, all managed by the National Trust, which also cares for the dramatic mine ruins at Wheal Coates, a short hike north along the Coast Path (see second photo).

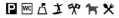

21 Trevaunance Cove, St Agnes

Lifeguarded and zoned for swimming and surfing, this has good facilities close to the beach. Access is a short walk from two convenient car parks. There are caves and rock pools to explore at low tide and a wealth of industrial history on the high cliffs above, among the stones on the beach and in St Agnes itself. Several illustrated beachside plaques describe the town's mining heritage.

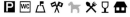

22 Trevellas Porth

This remote beach of pebbles and rocks with some sand is in a former industrial area dotted with engine houses, chimneys and spoil heaps. A short walk leads to the Blue Hills Visitor Centre, where tin is streamed, smelted and made into gifts. Please heed warning signs of strong currents. Do not swim.

11

23 Perranporth and Perran Sands (Penhale Sands)

As the tide recedes, Perran Sands joins Perranporth beach to form a vast 5 km (3 mile) long stretch of gold sand, backed by a huge area of sand dunes. Washed by long waves, the sands are lifeguarded and ideal for surfing, but also shallow and good for swimming. Naturists use the far end of the beach. Perranporth has a wide range of facilities.

🅿 🆆 ⛺ 🏕 🎿 🐕 ✕ 🍴 🏠 ♿

24 Holywell

A large, sandy beach backed by extensive dunes, popular with both families and surfers. Lifeguarded, it has good facilities, including a surf school. Access is via a 400 m level walk from the National Trust car park. Follow the Trust's large display map for local walks around the cliffs and commons to discover prehistoric sites and (only at low tide) a cave with a holy well.

🅿 🆆 ⛺ 🏕 🎿 🐕 ✕ 🍴 🏠

25 Porth Joke (Polly Joke)

This long, sandy beach is pleasantly secluded and unspoilt, even in summer, but calls for a ten minute walk from West Pentire or Cubert Common car parks. There are rock pools and caves to explore and the clifftops are famous for wildflowers, but please be aware strong currents can make swimming dangerous at times.

🅿 ⛺ 🐕 🍴

26 Crantock Beach, Newquay

A huge beach of golden sand backed by extensive dunes, and an important area for wildlife. Popular with families, it offers ample space for children to explore and play, or build sandcastles. It is known for surfing and has a school offering instruction and paddleboarding.

Crantock is bordered by the river Gannel, effectively a second, estuarine beach (second photo) but beware the river's currents, especially on strong tides, heed safety warnings and stay in lifeguarded areas.

27 Fistral Beach, Newquay

Famed as a surfing beach, it is also popular with families and zoned by the lifeguard. Fistral's beach complex includes a choice of places to eat and drink, surfing and clothes shops, a surf school, toilets and a large (pricey) car park with easy beach access. With so much to offer, Fistral is usually busy, but visitors can spread along 1 km (³/₄ mile) of golden sand.

28 Little Fistral Beach, Newquay

Tucked in below Towan Head, this beach of sand and shingle has its own quiet charm – but beware strong currents. Access from the convenient car park is via a short flight of steps. Fistral beach with its many facilities is a short, easy walk along the Coastpath. On the way, the ebbing tide uncovers patches of sand which make mini-beaches between the rocks.

29 Newquay Harbour (Slip Cove)

Newquay's picturesque historic harbour is a great place to watch fishing boats come and go, take a boat cruise to watch marine wildlife, or enjoy a boat fishing trip. It has a convenient car park and restaurant. The ebbing tide uncovers a very well sheltered arc of sand, but the whole harbour is dry at low tide.

🅿 ⓌⒸ ⛺ 🐎 ✕ ⚐ 🏠 ♿

30 Towan Beach, Newquay

At low tide Towan forms one long sandy beach with neighbouring Great Western, Tolcarne and Lusty Glaze beaches. Like them, it is family friendly and offers instruction and equipment hire in a variety of water-sports. Well sheltered and close to the town centre, it has good beachside facilities and a large aquarium. The nearest parking is ten minutes' walk away in Fore Street (short stay) or Newquay Harbour (long stay).

ⓌⒸ ⛺ ⛷ 🐎 ✕ ⚐ 🏠 ♿

31 Great Western Beach, Newquay

Newquay's original surfing beach, Great Western is family friendly with acres of golden sand. It's a good place to learn surfing and various watersports, including kayaking and paddleboarding, and to rent sports equipment. Visitors use Newquay's various public car parks and the access lane from Cliff Road (by the bus stop) as there is no beachside parking or vehicle access. Alternatively, walk from neighbouring Tolcarne or Towan beaches at low tide.

ⓌⒸ ⛺ 🏄 ⛷ 🐎 ✕ ⚐ 🏠

32 Tolcarne Beach, Newquay

A large family friendly, sandy beach with excellent beachside facilities, including a restaurant, cafe terrace, beach shop and surfing instruction/ hire. Although privately owned, it is fully open to the public, but parking is reserved for the beach-side accommodation. Non-residents must use Newquay's various public car parks and access the beach by a long flight of steps, a winding lane or, at low tide, walk over from neighbouring Lusty Glaze or Great Western beaches.

33 Lusty Glaze, Newquay

A fine sandy beach, sheltered by high cliffs. Access by a long flight of steps. The excellent facilities include a restaurant, beach shop, showers, changing rooms and an adventure centre offering equipment hire and instruction in a wide range of activities, such as surfing, jet skiing and boat tours. Privately owned, it is open to the public, except when closed for exclusive events. It offers free live music weekly and is a wedding venue.

34 Porth Beach, Newquay

A huge, well sheltered family beach of golden sand, with easy access and handy facilities. It's ideal for beach games, sandcastling, rockpooling and exploring. On the north side is Trevelgue Head, one of Cornwall's most impressive Iron Age cliff castles, which is also a prehistoric farming site and is fully accessible.

15

35 Whipsiderry Beach

A quiet beach of sand, shingle and rocks accessed by a long, steep flight of stairs, a complete contrast to Newquay's busy surfing beaches. As the tide recedes, it's a great place to escape the crowds, but beware unstable cliffs, strong undercurrents and being cut off by the returning tide. Limited roadside parking.

36 Watergate Bay

A huge sandy beach backed by cliffs, with good facilities and easy access. It is famed for surfing and offers surf hire and a surf shop, plus instruction in various watersports, including surfing, kitesurfing and paddleboarding. Lifeguarded with zones for special activities, it is also popular with families and dog walkers. As always, please heed warning notices of hazards, including rock falls and strong currents.

37 Mawgan Porth

A great family beach with rock pools and caves, also popular with surfers, with a surf shop and instruction. A vast expanse of golden sand at low tide, it is well sheltered with cliffs either side. The facilities are good, as is access.

38 Bedruthan Steps
One of the Cornish Coastpath's most impressive sights, a ten minute walk from Carnewas car park and tearooms. The steps to Bedruthan beach were closed at the time of writing due to a major rock-fall.

39 Pentire Steps
A large and beautiful beach of golden sand, but usually quiet and often deserted. For the agile and adventurous, and for experienced surfers, it's a 1 km (3/4 mile) walk from Park Head car park, followed by a steep zig-zag path and a final scramble over sometimes slippery rocks – but well worth it. Also, it is only accessible at lower stages of the tide. Beware of rip currents.

40 Porthcothan
Popular with swimmers and sun-bathers, sheltered by cliffs at high tide and backed by grassy dunes, at low tide it forms a huge sandy beach and connects with coves north and south. There is a handy beach café/shop.

41 Treyarnon Bay
A fine sandy beach, even at high tide, good for both families and surfers, it is zoned when the life-guard is active. Please observe the warning notices about hazardous areas of the beach. The car park, café, toilets and shop are all handy. Access is easy. There is good rock pooling.

42 Constantine Bay

A large, but exposed sandy beach with plenty of rock pools, it is well regarded by experienced surfers. Beware of rip currents, exposed rocks and the steep shelf at high tide. Limited parking: alternative parking at Treyarnon, ten minutes' walk along the Coast Path.

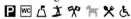

43 Booby's Bay

A fine though exposed beach of golden sand with good rock pools. Beware slippery rocks and strong currents. Park at Constantine Bay (alternative parking at Trevose Head and the north end of Booby's Bay) and follow the Coast Path. Access is by climbing down over rocks, or over the sand from Constantine Bay at low tide. Facilities at Constantine Bay.

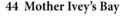

44 Mother Ivey's Bay

An attractive and sheltered beach sloping gently up to the cliffs, it is relatively quiet despite the nearby holiday park. The reason? A good twenty minute walk is needed from the main car parks at Harlyn Bay or Trevose Head, but there is a closer field car park with no facilities. Otherwise, facilities at Harlyn Bay and Constantine Bay.

18

45 Harlyn Bay

A large and popular beach of golden sand, ideal for families with its rock pools and dunes. It is lifeguarded in season and good for water sports and surfing (both novices and experienced surfers). Lessons are available in kayaking, coasteering, surfing and paddleboarding.

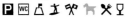

46 Trevone

Popular with both families and surfers, this is a large Blue Flag beach of golden sand with good facilities and disabled access. There is seasonal lifeguard cover, but avoid the right side of the beach because of strong currents.

West of the main beach, the aptly named Rocky Beach (Newtrain Bay) is great for exploring and rock pooling. Low tide reveals a large pool to bathe in.

47 Harbour Cove and Hawker's Cove

A huge sandy beach on the Camel estuary, with great views, Harbour Cove joins with Hawker's Cove and Gun Point at low tide. It is relatively quiet, ideal for exercising a dog, but there are no facilities and swimming is not recommended because of strong currents. Parking is a short walk away by Lellizzick, PL28 8HR, SW907774.

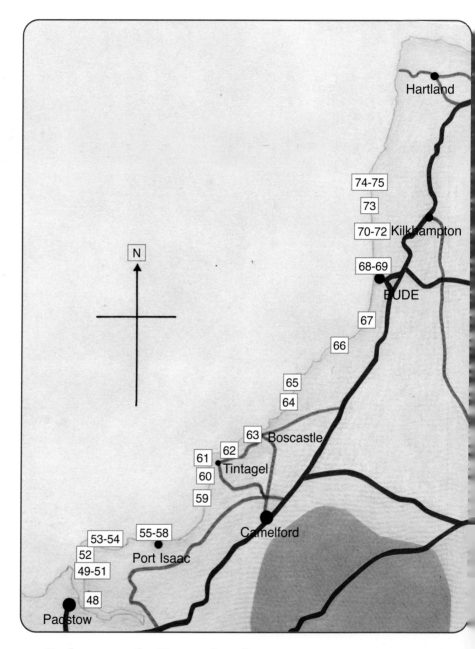

Padstow to the Devon border

Eastwards from the sheltered sandy beaches of the Camel estuary, Cornwall's north coast assumes an increasingly rugged character.

Rocky coves such as Tintagel Haven and Crackington Haven take what shelter they may from the implacable Atlantic waves. Other sheltered nooks among the cliffs are occupied by small, picturesque harbours: Port Quin, Port Isaac, Port Gaverne and Boscastle.

Beyond the fantastically contorted rocks of Millook beach the coast opens onto the wide golden sands of Widemouth and Bude. Famed for surfing, these are also great family beaches, but as everywhere on the north coast, the sea's strength must be respected.

Approaching Devon, the cliffs grow higher and steeper, interspersed with stream-cut valleys, opening onto the sea in a series of remote surf-washed, boulder-strewn beaches, with saw-toothed reefs.

With their waterfalls and rock pools, these beaches are for exploration – Nirvana for adventurous children and dogs.

48 Porthilly Cove

Low tide uncovers this beach of shingle and sand, making it continuous with Rock and Daymer Bay. It is much less visited than the neighbouring beaches, making it a pleasant place to relax or walk a dog. There is limited roadside parking near the church. Rock's facilities are a 1 km (3/4 mile) walk.

49 Rock

At low tide, Rock's sandy, dune-backed estuary beach stretches from Porthilly Cove (above) to Daymer Bay. It has good facilities within easy reach of the car park, including a ramp to the beach and the Padstow ferry.

Rock's waterfront activity centre offers water skiing, wakeboarding, paddleboarding, fishing trips and more. Please heed warnings of soft sand areas and strong currents, making it unsafe to swim out of your depth.

50 Daymer Bay

A gently sloping sandy beach on the Camel estuary, ideal for a long relaxing family day. Bathing is good, but take care with currents at low tide. It was celebrated by poet John Betjeman, who sleeps in the charming church of St Enodoc, a short walk across the dunes.

51 Trebetherick

Broadagogue beach is a good stretch of coarse sand and rocky reefs at low tide. Access is a 400m walk south along the Coast Path from Polzeath and steps down to the beach. Beware submerged rocks and currents here and at the rocky neighbouring Greenaway beach. Both beaches are good for a quiet rest or walking the dog. Facilities at Polzeath and Daymer Bay.

52 Polzeath

Popular with surfers and families alike, this Blue Flag beach has good facilities and disabled access. Low tide reveals a vast area of golden sand and gives easy access to the sister beach, New Polzeath.

53 Lundy Bay

Lundy Bay is a pleasant 15 minute walk from the small National Trust car park, plus steps and a scramble over rocks. It can get busy at low tide, which reveals plenty of sand and rockpools, but you may have Lundy to yourself as the tide comes in. Follow the upper path back to the car park to see Lundy Hole, a zawn, or collapsed sea cave.

P △ 🐕

54 Epphaven Cove

Follow the Coastpath east for five minutes from Lundy Bay to find Epphaven Cove. Access involves a scramble over slippery rocks. Again, low tide reveals a sandy cove which joins with Lundy at the bottom of the tide.

P △ 🐕

55 Port Quin

A small, unspoilt and sheltered cove of pebbles and rocks with sand at low tide, Port Quin is both family and dog friendly. It's well suited to swimming, rockpooling, paddleboarding, snorkelling and kayaking. Avoid the top of the tide, when the beach is submerged and arrive early on busy days because the car park (National Trust) is small, though convenient.

P △ 🐕

56 Pine Haven

This delightful little rocky inlet and small beach is a good place to relax, escape the crowd and enjoy a picnic. It calls for a little effort, being 700m (1/2 mile) west along the Coast Path from Port Isaac. Facilities at Port Isaac.

57 Port Isaac

A fishing village of real charm, sheltered in a rocky cove, Port Isaac's beautiful situation and houses built in local stone and slate have made it an ideal backdrop for films such as *Fisherman's Friends* and TV dramas from *Poldark* to *Doc Martin*. Low tide strands the fishing boats and reveals a beach of sand and rock pools.

58 Port Gaverne

A small, sheltered beach of shingle and rocks, with sand at low tide. Family and dog friendly, with a beachside pub and easy access, it has a school offering instruction and equipment hire in several water sports including paddle-boarding and kayaking. Parking by the beach is very limited: you may have to walk from Port Isaac's car parks.

59 Tregardock Beach

Known to a few surfers and walkers, this large beach of coarse sand and rocks is usually quiet and a great place to exercise a dog. It is only accessible at low tide after a 1 km (3/4 mile) descent of 140 m down a steep path. This is relieved by steps, but take care with the last section over potentially slippery rocks. Park carefully on the lane to Tregardock Farm near Treligga (SX 050848). Spaces are limited. Please avoid causing an obstruction.

60 Trebarwith Strand

There are good facilities and two car parks a moderate walk from the beach. Choose your time. The ebbing tide uncovers a huge beach of golden sand: the rising tide comes in fast, covering the sand and washing the rocks of the upper beach with strong waves (take care). The view from the Port William pub's outside tables can be very dramatic at high tide. Surfing is popular and there is a surfing school.

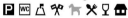

61 Tintagel Haven

This small sand and shingle cove is one for agile explorers since access is tricky and steep. It only appears as the tide drops, but has a dramatic waterfall and Merlin's Cave, which is 100 m long and passes under Tintagel Castle. Park at Tintagel (facilities) and follow the footpath towards the castle.

62 Bossiney Haven

This attractive beach, a short distance from Tintagel, was closed at the time of writing due to a major rock fall.

63 Boscastle Harbour

The only viable harbour on a long stretch of Cornwall's rocky north coast, Boscastle is well sheltered by high cliffs and two stone walls built in 1584. Today it is a haven for small fishing boats and leisure craft but it was was a bustling commercial port before the railway reached North Cornwall in 1893. Boscastle's picturesque quay and streets are lined with cafes, pubs and shops, as well as the Museum of Witchcraft and Magic and the National Trust shop/visitor centre.

Walks up the cliff to either side of the harbour reveal dramatic views.

64 The Strangles

This fine sand and shingle beach is located 1.5 km (1 mile) south of Crackington Haven and 100 m south of Trevigue. Reaching it involves a 1.1 km (3/4 mile) walk from the parking area (SX 135951) and a 150 m (495 ft) descent. The path is safe and relieved in parts by steps, but calls for some agility and effort, especially the last section. Consequently, the Strangles is never over-busy. It's a great place to relax and walk a dog, but not to swim.

65 Crackington Haven

Crackington Haven is surrounded by high, rugged cliffs, giving it some shelter on this exposed coast. Formerly a small port, it's good for families and surfers alike. Well provided with facilities, the beach is shingle at high tide, but low tide reveals sand and rock pools. Beware rip currents and reefs. Swim in lifeguarded area.

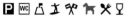

66 Millook

Composed mainly of large pebbles and coarse shingle, this isn't a bathing beach but it is well known among experienced surfers. Penhalt Cliff's dramatic folded sandstones and shales are late Carboniferous (c 345-280 million years old). Limited roadside parking at Millook. Alternative parking up on Penhalt cliff (SS188005).

🅿 👜 🐕

67 Widemouth

This 2 mile long Blue Flag beach of golden sand is popular with both families and surfers. There are several surf schools. The rockpooling is good too. There is a seasonal dog ban on part of the beach; dogs are permitted all year at the southern end. There is free parking on the cliffs at either end of the beach.

🅿 🚾 ⛺ 👜 🤸 🐎 🐕 ✕ 🏠

68 Summerleaze, Bude

A huge, sandy beach with room enough despite its popularity, it is easily accessible from Bude. The strong waves are suitable for surfing, not for children. However, the free tidal pool provides safe bathing. Bude's breakwater, protecting its small harbour, and the canal with its massive lock gates are worth exploring.

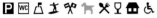

69 Crooklets (Bude)

Crooklets is a sandy, lifeguarded beach popular with both families and surfers. Its many facilities include a convenient car park, disabled access, showers, chalets, children's playground and surf school. Crooklets forms one long beach with Northcott at low tide: don't get cut off by the tide if you try walking this!

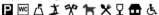

70 Northcott Mouth

Low tide uncovers the sand beyond the shingle and rock pools, which have to be clambered over. It is similar in nature to neighbouring Sandymouth and Duckpool beaches. All three are well managed by the National Trust. Swimming is advised only in the lifeguarded area and there is a separate surfing zone. Beware cliff falls, currents and submerged rocks, especially at high tide.

29

71 Sandymouth

Popular with both surfers and rockpoolers, this is a shingle and rock beach, with a large area of fine sand as the tide recedes. It benefits from good facilities. Access is by a 200 m path and a few steps. Beware currents, rocks submerged by the tide and cliff falls (as at Northcott and Duckpool).

72 Duckpool

The most northerly in the trio of fine shingle, rock and sand beaches, it lies at the end of a lovely, steep sided combe and reveals its fascinating rockpools and its golden sand as the tide recedes. Having fewer facilities and no lifeguard, it is less busy than its two southerly neighbours. The same cautions about cliff falls and submerged rocks apply. Avoid swimming because of rip currents.

73 Stanbury Mouth

This is a wilder, rockier, more remote version of Duckpool. It's great for rockpooling and walking a dog, but not for swimming. Access requires a twenty minute walk, plus a spirit of adventure and some agility, especially in the last, steep section over stream-washed rocks, but you may well have the beach to yourself. Park at the end of the lane beyond Stanbury (SS 205135). Take the PUBLIC FOOTPATH left. Turn right at the junction and follow the path down to the beach.

74 Marsland Mouth

A beautiful and secluded rocky beach astride the Cornwall-Devon border, set amid dramatic cliff scenery and washed, by powerful Atlantic waves. It requires a tough 1km walk from Welcombe to reach it and has no facilities. Enjoy the solitude, sea and birds, beware of crumbling cliffs and rock falls.

75 Welcombe Mouth

At high tide the surf roars over the pebbles at Welcombe, which is just on the Devon side of the border. As the tide drops, long rocky ridges appear, and a little sand. High cliffs and a pretty waterfall add to Welcombe's charm. Access is by a short, steep path from the car park (SS214179), itself reached by a narrow lane and a rough track.

Tourist Information Centres

Boscastle 01840 250010
Bude 01288 354240
Hayle 01736 754399
Newquay 01637 838516
Padstow 01841 533449

Penzance 01736 335530
Perranporth 01872 575254
St Agnes 01872 554150
St Ives 01736 796297

Some other Bossiney books you might find useful

Cornwall beach and cove guide – South coast (in preparation)
Devon beach and cove guide

Shortish walks near the Land's End
Really short walks – West Cornwall
Really short walks – St Ives to Padstow
Writers' walks on the Cornish coast
Really short walks – North Cornwall
Shortish walks – North Cornwall

Discover North Cornwall
About Tintagel

For a full list of Bossiney books, see www.bossineybooks.com